The Pei

WORCESTER COLL

Holidays

Gill Tanner and Tim Wood

Photographs by Maggie Murray

Illustrations by Pat Tourret

A & C Black · London

Here are some of the people you will meet in this book.

The Hart family in 1990

The Cook family in 1960

Lee Hart is the same age as you.
His sister Kerry is eight years old.
What is Lee's mum called?

This is Lee's mum Linda when she
was just nine years old in 1960.
She is with her mum and dad,
her brother and her baby sister.

The Smith family in 1930

Richard Smith

Lucy Smith

May

Jack and June

The Barker family in 1900

Charles Barker

Alice Barker

Fred

Amy and Adam

Harry

Lucy

This is Lee's granny June when she was just a baby in 1930. Her brother Jack is looking after her.

This is Lee's great grandma Lucy when she was six years old in 1900. Can you see what her sister and her brothers are called?

3

How many differences can you spot
between these two photographs?

One shows modern people on holiday
and the other shows people on holiday
one hundred years ago.

This book is about holidays.

It will help you find out how
holidays have changed
in the last hundred years.

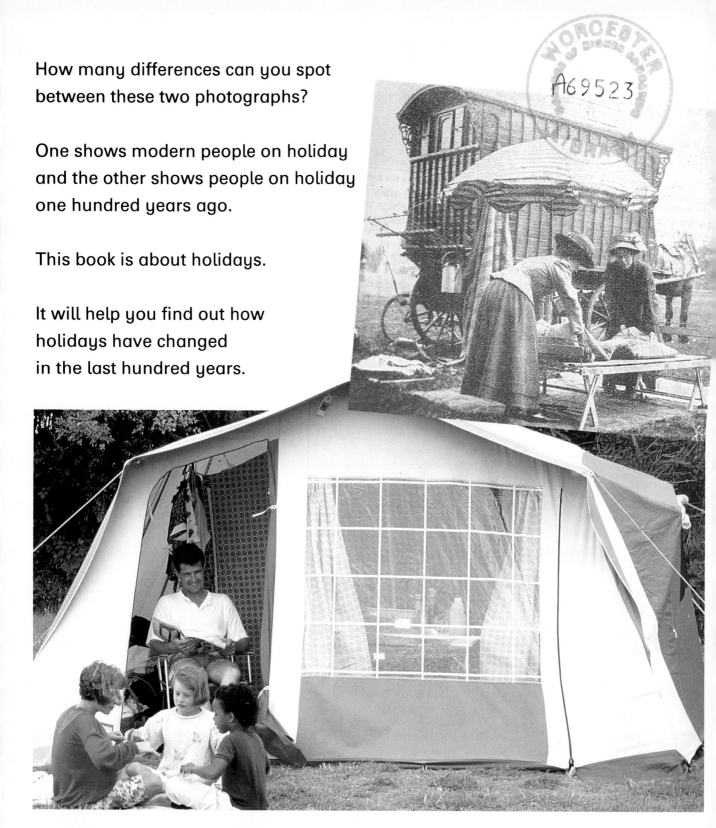

There are more than twenty mystery objects in this book
and you can find out what they are.
They will tell you a lot about people in the past.

In 1900 most girls wore one of these
when the weather was hot.
It is made of thin cotton.
It is big enough to cover a page of this book.
Can you guess what it is?

Turn the page to find out.

Can you find the mystery object in this picture?

It is a **sun bonnet**.

The Barker children spent the summer holidays
on a farm.

They helped gather in the harvest.

When the sun was hot
Amy and Lucy both wore sun bonnets.

Fred wore a floppy sun hat.

In 1900 most parents thought that
sunshine was dangerous.

They and their children wore hats in sunny weather
to protect them from sunburn and headaches.

This mystery object is made of metal.
It is the same size as a large spoon.
In 1900 it was used to serve something cold
which the Barker children loved to eat.
Can you guess what it was used for?

Turn the page to find out.

Alice Barker has taken the older children
to the zoo as a treat.
Can you spot the mystery object?
It's an **ice-cream scoop**.

In those days ice-cream was not made in factories
and sold in packets or wrappers.
Ice-cream sellers made their own ice-cream.
They sold the ice cream from hand carts full of ice
which they pushed round the streets.
They served the ice-cream on paper sheets or saucers.
The Barkers called ice-creams 'penny licks'.
Can you see why?

This mystery object is made of canvas.

It is a bit longer than one of your arms.

The picture and writing on the front are big clues.

Amy Barker wore this at the seaside.

You may have used something like it

but yours might be made of plastic.

Can you guess what it is?

Turn the page to find out.

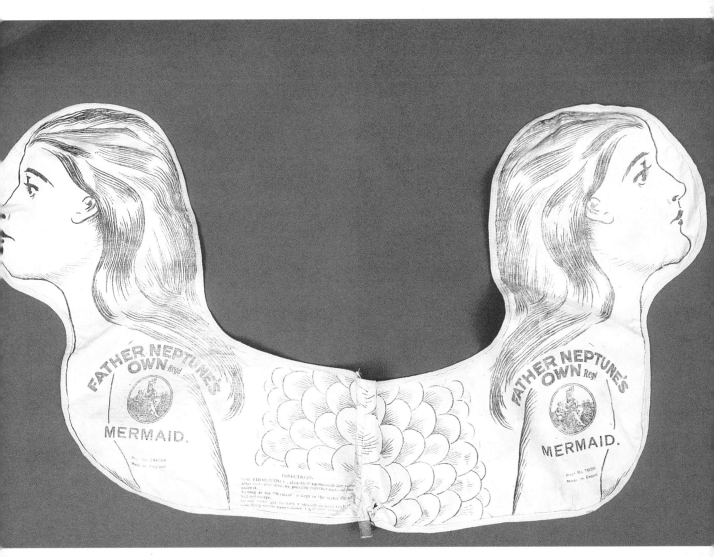

The Barker family are having a day at the seaside.
Amy can't swim yet
so she wears canvas **water wings** in the sea.
Before she began to blow them up,
she had to make the canvas wet
so the air would not leak out.

In those days lots of people went to the seaside
for day trips, especially on bank holidays.
They travelled there by train.
Most people wore their ordinary clothes on the beach.
They often used umbrellas to keep off the sun.
What other things can you see on this beach
that you wouldn't see on your seaside holidays?

10

All these mystery objects are made of metal.

The Smiths used them on holiday in 1930.

You can probably guess what one of them is.

That gives you a big clue about
the size of the objects.

They fit together in a clever way.

Can you guess what the Smiths used them for?

Turn the page to find out.

The Smith family are having a picnic.
Richard is using a **camping stove** and a **kettle**
to make a cup of tea.
Jack filled the kettle with water from the stream
while Richard lit the burner on the stove.
Richard will clip the kettle safely on to the stove
so it cannot fall off.

In the 1930s many families enjoyed
days out in the countryside.
There were no proper picnic areas.
Most people picnicked in fields.
The Smiths always asked the farmer first
before they set out their picnic.

This mystery object belonged to Lucy Smith.
It is made of metal, glass and leather.
You could easily carry it in one hand.
Lucy took it with her on all her holidays.
It helped her remember where she had been.
Can you guess what it is?

Turn the page to see if you are right.

Lucy has taken the children to London.
Can you spot the mystery object?
It's a **pocket camera**.

In those days many cameras
were too big to carry around easily.
This camera folded into a flat box for carrying.
When Lucy wanted to take a photograph
she unclipped the front lid of the camera.
Can you see how the camera folded and unfolded?

14

Jack Smith wore this mystery object at the seaside.
You may have one something like it.
But you would hate to wear this one
because it is made of very prickly wool.
Do you know what it is?

Turn the page to find out.

The Smith family are at the seaside.
Can you spot the mystery object?
It's Jack's **swimsuit**.

Lucy bought Jack's swimsuit in a shop
but she knitted swimsuits for her other children.
Almost everyone had woollen swimsuits in those days
although they were very uncomfortable to wear.
Woollen swimsuits itched when they were dry
and stretched when they got wet.
They took ages to dry out after swimming
and soon lost their shape.
Do you know what your swimsuit is made of?

These mystery objects belonged to Linda Cook in the 1960s

They are all made of metal.

Each one is about the same size as a 50p coin.

Look very closely.

You may spot a clue on each of the objects.

Do you have anything like them?

Can you guess what they are?

Turn the page to find out.

The Cook family is at a Butlin's holiday camp.

Linda is talking to a Redcoat.

Can you spot the mystery objects?

They are **badges**.

Each badge comes from a different Butlin's camp.

In the 1960s lots of families with young children
went to Butlin's holiday camps.

Each holiday-maker was given a Butlin's badge.

Linda's parents gave her their badges.

Linda swapped her spare badges
with her friends who went to other camps.

She soon had a big collection.

What do you collect from your holidays?

The mystery object on the right is made of plastic.

It belonged to Linda Cook.

The one on the left is made of straw.

It belonged to June Cook.

Linda and June bought them on holiday.

You can probably guess what these objects are.

But do you know where they come from?

And what have they to do with holidays?

Turn the page to find out.

The Cook family are back from their holidays in Spain.
They are going through customs.
Can you spot the mystery objects?
They are a **Spanish doll** and a **straw donkey**.

CUSTOMS

During the 1960s lots of people
went on package holidays abroad.
They went by aeroplane to countries like Spain
where the weather was hot and hotels were cheap.
People brought presents and souvenirs back with them.
Have you been abroad?
Where did you go?
What souvenirs did you bring back?

Now that you know a bit more about holidays
and how they have changed
over the last hundred years,
see if you can guess
what this mystery object is.

REG'D DESIGN
No. 727,258

It was used by ice-cream sellers
in 1930.
It is made of metal.
The little lever on the side
moved to make the container deeper.
What do you think was put in it?
What do you think it is?

You will find the answer on page 24.

Time-Line

These pages show you the objects in this book and the objects we use for holidays nowadays.

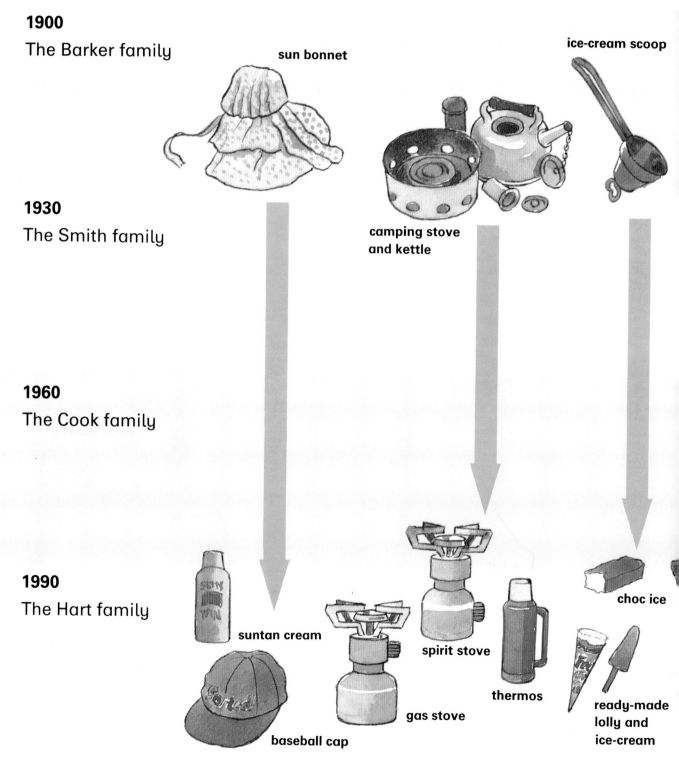

1900
The Barker family

sun bonnet

ice-cream scoop

1930
The Smith family

camping stove and kettle

1960
The Cook family

1990
The Hart family

suntan cream

baseball cap

gas stove

spirit stove

thermos

choc ice

ready-made lolly and ice-cream

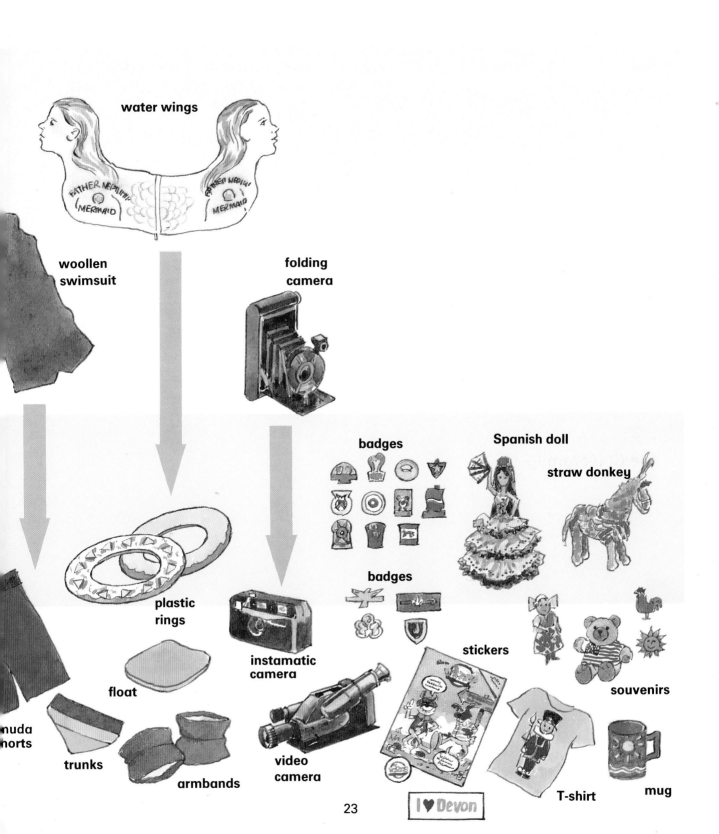

water wings

woollen swimsuit

folding camera

woollen swimsuit

badges

Spanish doll

straw donkey

plastic rings

badges

instamatic camera

stickers

souvenirs

float

muda horts

trunks

armbands

video camera

T-shirt

mug

I ♥ Devon

Index

The **mystery object** on page 21 is an **ice-cream wafer maker** used when June Smith was a child. A wafer biscuit fitted into the box. Ice-cream was pushed in on top. A second wafer was put on top. Then the ice-cream 'sandwich' was tipped out on to paper.

For parents and teachers

More about the objects and pictures in this book

Pages 5/6 Helping on the farm was a common holiday activity for poorer families and in certain seasons could cause wholesale absenteeism in rural areas. Suntans were not only considered dangerous but also unfashionable among the middle and upper classses because they were the hallmark of manual workers.

Pages 7/8 Ice-cream was first made in Britain in 1686. Biscuit cones reached Britain from Italy in about 1910. The key on the metal scoop shown turned two brass strips which pushed out the ice-cream.

Pages 9/10 Paddling was the most common water sport in 1900 and not many people could swim. Notice the lead stopper to keep the air from leaking out of the water wings.

Pages 11/12 Small clips on the wind shield supported the kettle over the methylated spirit burner. The kettle packed inside the circular metal wind shield.

Pages 13/14 This Kodak Vest Pocket Camera retracted to become about 2.5 cm thick. The viewfinder is the prism-shaped device attached to the lens. The operation and film winding were all done by hand. Only black and white film was available at this time. Colour film was invented in 1904 but was not widely used until after 1945.

Pages 15/16 Swimming costumes were usually made of knitted wool or serge. Nylon was invented in 1937 but nylon swimming costumes did not become widely available until the 1950s.

Pages 17/18 In 1906 Dodd's Socialist Holiday Camp, the first mixed, self-catering, permanent holiday camp, was opened at Caister-on-Sea in Norfolk.

Pages 19/20 Package holidays, made possible by the advent of cheap air travel, took off during the 1950s when about 2 million Britons went abroad annually.

Things to do

History Mysteries will provide an excellent starting point for all kinds of history work. There are lots of general ideas which can be drawn out of the pictures, particularly in relation to the way medical holidays, clothes, family size and lifestyles have changed in the last 100 years. Below are some starting points and ideas for follow up activities.

1 Work on families and family trees can be developed from the family on pages 2/3, bearing in mind that many children do not come from two-parent, nuclear families.

2 Find out more about holidays in in the past from a variety of sources, including interviews with older people in the community, books, museums, old postcards and photographs. Holidays weren't the same for everyone. Why not?

3 There is one object which is in one picture of the 1900s, one picture of the 1930s, and one picture of the 1960s. Can you find it?

4 Make a local study of your nearest seaside town or holiday centre and/or arrange a field trip to a museum which has old holiday exhibits, such as Woodspring Museum in Weston-super-Mare.

5 Look at the difference between the photographs and the illustrations in this book. What different kinds of things can they tell you?

6 Make your own collection of holiday objects, pictures or postcards. You can build up an archive or school museum over several years by encouraging children to bring in old objects, collecting unwanted items from parents – such as souvenirs from previous holidays – and collecting from junk shops and jumble sales. You may also be able to borrow handling collections from your local museum or library service.

7 Encouraging the children to look at the objects is a useful start, but they will get more out of this if you organise some practical activities which help to develop their powers of observation. These might include drawing the objects, describing an object to another child who must then pick out the object from the collection, or writing descriptions of the objects for labels or for catalogue cards.

8 Encourage the children to answer questions. What do the objects look and feel like? What are they made of? What makes them work? How old are they? How could you find out more about them? Do they do the job they are supposed to do?

9 What do the objects tell us about the people who used them? Children might do some writing, drawing or role play imagining themselves as the users of different objects.

10 Children might find a mystery object in their own house or school for the others to draw, write about and identify. Children can compare the objects in the book with objects in their own home or school.

11 If you have an exhibition, try pairing old objects with their nearest modern counterparts. Talk about each pair. Some useful questions might be: How can you tell which is older? Which objects have changed most over time? Why? What do you think of the older objects? What would people have thought of them when they were new? Can you test how well the objects work? Is the modern version better than the old version?

12 Make a time-line using your objects. You might find the time-line at the back of this book useful. You could include pictures in your time-line and other markers to help the children gain a sense of chronology. Use your time-line to bring out the elements of *change* (eg. the gradual development of holidays for all, the growing importance of package holidays abroad, the health implications of leisure and exposure to sunlight, different forms of holidays and holiday transport) and *continuity* (eg. the continuing need for rest and relaxation, school holidays, the lasting popularity of the seaside, souvenirs and postcards).

First published 1994
A & C Black (Publishers) Limited
35 Bedford Row, London WC1R 4JH

ISBN 0-7136-3800-1

A CIP catalogue record for this book is available
from the British Library.

Acknowledgements

The authors and publishers would like to thank Suella Postles and the staff of
Brewhouse Yard Museum, Nottingham; Mrs Tanner's Tangible History;
Yvonne Holland; Linda Maltman

Photographs by Maggie Murray except for p.4 (top) Ulrike Preuss/Format

Filmset by Rowland Phototypesetting Limited, Bury St Edmunds, Suffolk
Printed and bound in Italy by L.E.G.O.